Feel Good

Practice Journal

Feel Good Practice Journal

A COMPANION FOR MUSICIANS OF ALL KINDS

Elizabeth Wright & Casey Lipka

ISBN-13 979-8-218-26841-1

Book Design by Meredith Alden Lewis

This journal belongs to:

Contents

Introduction

Hello and welcome to the **Feel Good Practice Journal**!

We are Elizabeth & Casey, two musicians who are passionate about bringing loving attention to the practice room.

The independent time you spend with your instrument is personal and special. You may approach this time with any number of feelings or associations – fun, curiosity, creativity, expectation, anxiety... the list goes on.

No matter what feelings accompany you to the practice room or what associations you have, this journal meets you where you are. The **Feel Good Practice Journal** is about the process of looking and noticing, using neutrality as a starting point to cultivate a nurturing mindset with your craft.

The following pages lead you, through guided reflections and prompts, to develop a mindful and benevolent awareness, not only of your playing, but also of yourself. They provide a supportive backdrop for deep engagement, attention to your wellbeing, and fulfillment in the process of practicing. One question at a time, the doors of possibility, change, and transformation will open.

See you in the practice room!

Elizabeth & Casey

Why a journal?

We've created a journal, rather than a guide or manual, because we believe in the knowledge that's already within you. The spaciousness of these pages puts the power in your hands to observe, explore, and modify your practice in whatever way best serves you.

The journal is formatted so you can come back again and again, picking up where you left off, no matter how long it's been since you were last here.

For additional resources and support around practicing, please visit our website:

www.feelgoodpracticejournal.com

How do I use this journal?

We invite you to come to this journal as you are.

Each page is an invitation to spend time with yourself and your craft, to be fully present, and to develop and inhabit the creative practice that feels right for you.

So make the journal your own. Write as much or as little as you like. Use the blank space in whatever way best serves you, whether that is to plan, dream, doodle, or document your day-to-day thoughts and revelations.

We encourage you to go at your own pace. No matter the day, you will find warmth and acceptance in these pages.

Let's go!

Week 1

Start Here

Date ______________

What brought you to music?

Start Here ______________________________

Practice Notes

Date ______________

When you think of music, what brings you joy?

Start Here ______________________________

Practice Notes

Date ____________________

What is something you do well in your musical life?

Start Here ____

Practice Notes

Date ____________

What is one meaningful memory you've experienced in music?

Start Here ____________________________

Practice Notes

Date ____________

When you think of your music, what feels disconnected or needs work?

Start Here ______________________

Practice Notes

Date ______________________

What gets in the way of your playing?

Start Here ____

Practice Notes

Date ____________________

What does your musical dream look like? If nothing could stop you, what would you do?

Start Here ____

Practice Notes

Week 2

Purpose

This section is an invitation to get intentional.

The following questions will help you name what you want, provide space for your vision to take shape, and ground you as you embark on the rest of the journal.

Date ____________

What brought you to this journal?

Purpose ____________________________

Date ____________________

What's the purpose of this journal for you?

Purpose ____

Practice Notes

Date ___________

What would you like to get out of this journal?
Why is that important?

Purpose ___________________________________

Date ______________________

What barriers or challenges do you anticipate as you use this journal?

Purpose ____

Practice Notes

Date ___

What support (e.g. people, tools, physical space, written resources) do you need to put in place for yourself?

Purpose ___

Practice Notes

Date ________________

How would you like to feel, or what intention would you like to set (e.g. attitude, pace, energy) as you walk through the experience of this journal?

Purpose ________________________________

Practice Notes

Date ______________________

Imagine you've just completed the journal. You feel really good about your music and the progress you've made.

Describe in detail what this looks like. What is happening? What does your future self think, feel, or believe? What do they see?

Purpose ____

Practice Notes

Check-In

Notice and acknowledge how you are right now, this very moment.

Take stock – physically, psychologically, energetically – and allow whatever is there to be there.

Whoever you are today, however you feel, welcome.

Date ______________

How are you doing today?

Check-In ______________________________

Practice Notes

Date ______________

What's your energy level on a scale of 1 to 10?
How is your energy impacting how you show up for practice today?

Check-In ______________

Practice Notes

Date ______________________

How are you feeling as you come to the practice session today?

Check-In ____

Practice Notes

Date ______________________

Describe your energy as you enter the practice space.

Check-In ____

Practice Notes

Date ____________________

How are you feeling about playing music today?

Check-In ____

Practice Notes

Date ______________

How does your energy level affect your practice?

Check-In ______________________________

Practice Notes

Date ______________________

What state of mind are you in right now?
What state of mind would you like to be in?

Check-In ______________________________________

Practice Notes

Date ____________________

What kind of energy would you like to cultivate today?

Check-In ____

Date ______________

How do you feel physically or emotionally at this moment?

Check-In ______________

Being Present & Letting Go

What are you holding on to?

Take the opportunity to name and let go of what isn't serving you.

Date ________________

What do you need to let go of (e.g. to-do list; distractions; feelings, judgments, etc.) to be fully present today?

Practice Notes

Date ____________________

Take a moment before you play. What is something you can do to center yourself? *(E.g. take some deep breaths, take in the room around you, look out the window, close your eyes...)*

Practice Notes

Date ____________________

What do you need to name or acknowledge before you start practicing today?

Date ____________________

Take a deep breath and listen to what you need right now. Name it.

Practice Notes

Date ____________________

What is something you're grateful for today?

Practice Notes

Date ____________________

What distractions are present, externally or internally?
What commitment do you want to make to yourself about those distractions?

Practice Notes

Date ______________________

Close your eyes and name what helpful internal resources you can tap into today. *(E.g. focus, kindness, bravery, presence...)*

Practice Notes

Week 5

Physical Awareness

Bring a kind awareness to your physicality to awaken presence and connection.

Date ____________________

Take a moment to scan your body. What do you observe?

Practice Notes

Date ______________________

What do you want to be aware of in your body as you practice today?

Physical Awareness ________________________________

Date ____________

What parts of your body seem to want your attention right now? What do they need?

Physical Awareness ____________

Practice Notes

Date ______________

What physical tendencies would you like to stay aware of today? What tightness or discomfort is present?

Physical Awareness ______________________________

Practice Notes

Date ______________

What could you do to bring more ease to your body? How could you feel more free?

Physical Awareness ______________

Date ________________

What physical sensations are drawing your attention?
How would you like to be attentive to them in your practice?

Practice Notes

Date ____________________

What do you notice in your body before you play?
What physical adjustments would you like to make before beginning practice?

Physical Awareness ______________________________

Practice Notes

Date ______________

What nourishment might you need for your body before you start practice?

Physical Awareness ______________________________

Practice Notes

Week 6

Intention

Setting an intention gives you an empowered choice about the way you want to exist, feel, and interact.

That may be a word or phrase that grounds you in the present, inspires you, or embodies something you want to cultivate.

Over time, intention-setting enables you to mindfully foster a way of being that supports you and your craft.

Date ____________________

What headspace would you like to foster for your practice session? *(E.g. I want to foster curiosity, calm, ease, focus, presence, perseverance, playfulness...)*

Intention ____

Date ____________________

What feelings would you like to nurture throughout your practice session? (E.g. I want to feel grounded, joyful, self-assured, optimistic, awesome, loving, serene, thankful, trusting...)

Intention ____

Practice Notes

Date ___________________

How would you like to be in this practice session? What words come to mind? (E.g. curious, calm, confident, empowered, easeful, free...)

Intention ____

Date ____________________

How would a child tell you to approach this practice session?
(E.g. taking it easy, making it creative...)

Intention ____

Date ____________________

How would you like to be present for yourself today?
What internal qualities would be beneficial? (E.g. focus, attitude, beliefs about yourself...)

Intention ____

Date ____________________

What are three words that reflect how you'd like to be throughout your practice today?

Intention ____

Practice Notes

Date ____________________

Set an intention for your practice today.
(E.g. How would you like to approach your session? What ways of being would support you?)

Intention ____

Practice Notes

Week 7

Reflection

The following pages provide space to check in, look back, and revisit why you're here.

Date ______________

What is working for you in your practice? What's not?

Reflection ______________________________

Practice Notes

Date ____________________

What do you want to continue working on?

Reflection ____

Date ____________________

What do you notice in your body when you play?

Reflection ____________________

Practice Notes

Date ____________________

What observations are you making or have you made about how you practice?

Reflection ____

Practice Notes

Date ______________________

What "a-ha" moments have you had?

Reflection ____

Date ___________________

Reflect on your original intention for starting this journal. Are you still aligned with your purpose? (Return to the *Purpose* section on page 32 to revisit your original answers.)

Reflection ____

Practice Notes

Date ______________

Has anything surprised you throughout the experience of this journal? What has changed?

Reflection ______________________________

Date ____________________

How has the act of showing up with this journal impacted your music?

Reflection ____

Practice Notes

Date ______________________

What is the biggest change you've noticed since you started this journal?

Reflection ________________________________

Week 8

Acknowledgment

Take a moment to acknowledge yourself, celebrate your wins, and shine a light on what feels good.

Date ___________________

Name at least one win you've had this week!

Acknowledgment ___________________________________

Practice Notes

Date ____________________

What is something you're proud of about today's session?

Acknowledgment ____

Practice Notes

Date __________________

What do you want to celebrate about your playing?

Acknowledgment ______________________________

Practice Notes

Date ___________________

Shine a light on something you feel good about this week!

Acknowledgment ________________________________

Date ______________________

How can you honor and uplift yourself today?

Acknowledgment ______________________________________

Practice Notes

Date ___

What are three things you're grateful for?

Acknowledgment ___

Practice Notes

Date ______________________

What do you want to acknowledge about how you've walked through this journal thus far?

Acknowledgment ____

Practice Notes

Date ______________________

How will you celebrate the progress you've made with this journal? *(E.g. share your experience with someone, go out to dinner, order a fancy coffee, throw a party!)*

Acknowledgment ______________________________________

Week 9

Completion

Congratulations!

You've arrived at the final installment of this journal.

Reflect on the journal experience, consider how it has impacted you, and explore what you might take with you in the next chapter of your musical journey.

Date ______________________

What have you noticed about yourself as you've gone through this journal experience?

Completion ______________________________________

Practice Notes

Date ____________________

How has the self-reflective process in this journal affected the way you see yourself, your instrument, or your creative process?

Completion ____

Practice Notes

Date ____________________

What has changed about you/your practice over the course of this journal?

Completion ____________________

Practice Notes

Date ______________________

What about the journaling process worked for you? What would you like to take with you moving forward?

Completion ____

Practice Notes

Date ____________________

Moving forward, what personal practices (e.g. healthy eating habits, sleep, meditation, down time, going through this journal again) would support your artistry?

Completion ____________________

Practice Notes

Date ______________

What external support *(e.g. a mentor, teacher, workshop, collaboration)* *would you like to put in place for the next phase of your musical journey?*

Completion ______________________________

Practice Notes

Date ____________________

What internal resources (e.g. dedication, patience, courage, ease, presence) would you most like to tap into for the next phase of your musical journey?

Completion ____

Practice Notes

Date ______________________

How will you celebrate the completion of this journal?

Completion ____

Practice Notes

Notes